Compiled by Joan Frey Boytim

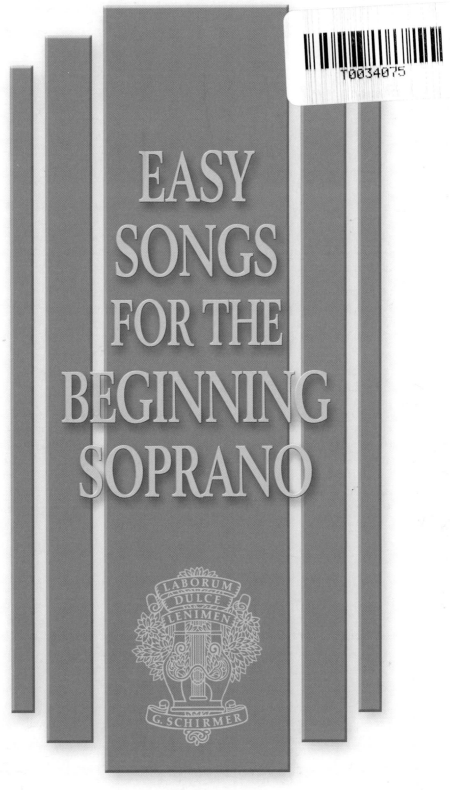

EASY
SONGS
FOR THE
BEGINNING
SOPRANO

Laura Ward, pianist

Larry Rock, engineer
Recorded May 2000, Settlement Music School, Germantown, Pennsylvania

ISBN 978-0-634-01968-5

G. SCHIRMER, Inc.

DISTRIBUTED BY

7777 W. BLUEMOUND RD. P.O. BOX 13819 MILWAUKEE, WI 53213

To access companion recorded piano accompaniments online, visit:
www.halleonard.com/mylibrary

Enter Code
1760-0313-2823-1222

PREFACE

Easy Songs for Beginning Singers will appeal to the middle school age group as well as to many beginning high school, college, and adult students. There are between 22 and 24 songs in each book with online accompaniments included.

Suitable vocal repertoire for the middle school student taking voice lessons has been rather sparse. For many years, most young people did not begin vocal study until the ninth or tenth grade level or even later. There was a misconception that it was a dangerous practice to study voice at an earlier age. As teachers have become more knowledgeable, as students are maturing much earlier, and as musicals are being produced in the middle schools, one finds many young people beginning lessons in the seventh and eighth grades and even earlier.

The foreign language texts have been purposely eliminated to make the songs very easy to learn. Modification has been made to the dated English versions and, in some cases, new texts have been provided. The songs are quite short and they generally have rather moderate tessituras. The maximum ranges, explored in only a few selections, are C to G for soprano, A to E for mezzo, C to F-sharp for tenor, and A-flat to E-flat for baritone. Most songs do not use those extended ranges.

A number of the songs will not be familiar but should prove to be a welcome addition to well known repertoire published in these collections. At the same time, I have included a few popular standards in each volume. Songs in the female books explore many folk songs and interesting translated French bergerettes and early German lieder. The male volumes each contain a number of English and American folksongs, spirituals, and several art songs. There are several quite humorous songs in each of the books.

Most of the accompaniments are suitable for student pianists. A few songs in each volume will be more of a challenge to lead the student directly into Schirmer's *First Book of Solos* and *First Book of Solos Part II*.

Birth and death dates for composers have been included whenever possible. These dates are simply not known for a few of the composers, particularly minor musical figures who had few published works. In lieu of birth and death dates, publication dates are provided, when known, to allow a teacher or student at least some chronological perspective for a song.

It is my hope that these four volumes will provide a new and worthwhile source of music for the novice singer of any age, as well as a fun collection for the more experienced student of voice.

Joan Frey Boytim

BIOGRAPHY

Compiler Joan Frey Boytim is a nationally recognized expert in teaching beginning voice students and has conducted workshops, seminars, and master classes across the United States. She is the compiler of the widely used series *The First Book of Solos, The First Book of Solos Part II, The Second Book of Solos,* and *The First Book of Broadway Solos.*

CONTENTS

The price of this publication includes access to companion recorded piano accompaniments online, for download or streaming, using the unique code found on the title page. Visit **www.halleonard.com/mylibrary** and enter the access code.

Alice Blue Gown

Joseph McCarthy

Harry Tierney
1890-1965

Tenderly

I once had a gown it was
lit - tle silk-worms that made

al - most new, Oh, the dain - ti - est thing, it was sweet Al - ice Blue, With
silk for that gown, Just __ made that much silk and then crawled in the ground, For there

lit - tle for - get - me - nots placed here and there, When I had it on, I
nev - er was an - y - thing like it be - fore, And I don't dare to hope there will

walked on the air, And it wore, and it wore, and it wore, _____ Till it
be - an - y - more, But it's gone 'cause it just had to be, _____ Still it

Moderate waltz

went and it was - n't no more. _____ In my sweet lit - tle
wears in my mem - o - ry. _____

Al - ice blue gown, _____ when I first wan - dered down in - to

town, _____ I was both proud and shy, as I felt ev - 'ry eye, but in

ev - 'ry shop win - dow I'd primp, pass - ing by, Then in man - ner of fash - ion I'd

frown _____ And the world seemed to smile all a - round, _____ till it

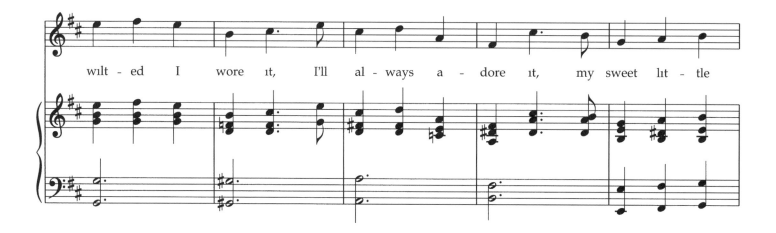

wilt - ed I wore it, I'll al - ways a - dore it, my sweet lit - tle

Al - ice blue gown   The   gown _____

April Showers

B.G. DeSylva

Louis Silvers
1889-1954

Though A - pril show - ers _____ may come your way, _____ They bring the

flow - ers _____ that bloom in May _____ So if it's

rain - ing, _____ have no re - grets, _____ Be - cause it

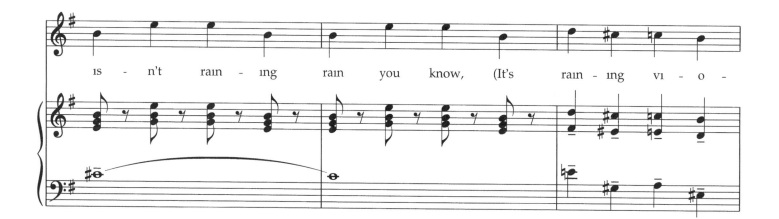

is - n't rain - ing rain you know, (It's rain - ing vi - o -

lets,) And where you see clouds _____ up - on the hills, _____

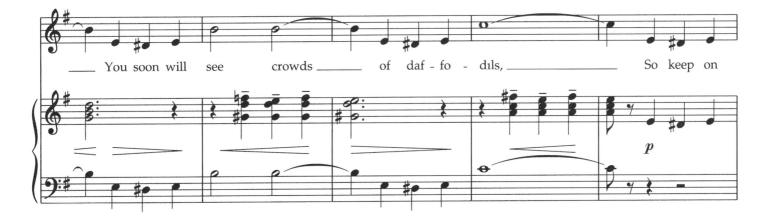

_____ You soon will see crowds _____ of daf - fo - dils, _____ So keep on

look - ing for a blue - bird And lis - t'ning for his song, When - ev - er A - pril

show - ers come a - long   long _____

Butterflies
(Der Schmetterling)

English text by
Paul England

Johann Abraham Peter Schulz
1747-1800
arranged by Heinrich Reimann
1850-1906

Poco allegretto

Be-side a brook one sum-mer's day There flew a paint-ed but-ter-fly; Its co-lor caught a maid-en's eye Who ea-ger ran to seize the prey, Who ea-ger ran to seize the

prey   She ea-ger ran to seize the prey.   But

in her ar-dor none too wise The mai-den stum-bled sad to tell, And

in the wa-ter straight she fell, And in the wa-ter straight she

fell   Yes, in the wa-ter straight she fell! She screamed,

a hunt - er heard the maid And ran to lend his time - ly aid, He

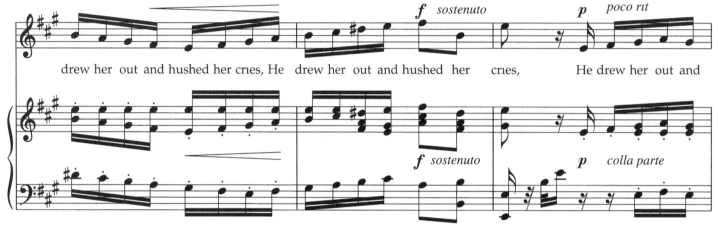

drew her out and hushed her cries, He drew her out and hushed her cries, He drew her out and

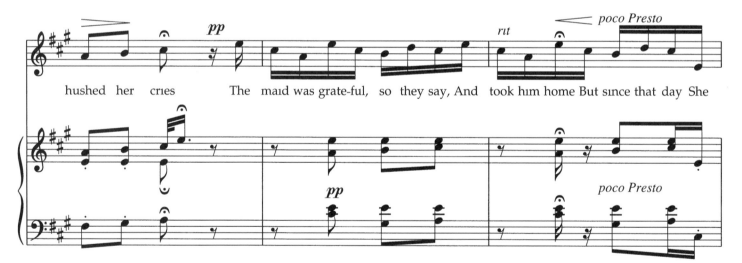

hushed her cries The maid was grate-ful, so they say, And took him home But since that day She

has no time for but - ter - flies, She has no time for but - ter - flies

Cradle Song
(Wiegenlied)

English text by
Arthur Westbrook

Johannes Brahms
1833-1897

With gentle motion

1. Lul-la-by and good night! With
2. Lul-la-by and good night! Those

stars shin-ing bright, Creep in-to your bed, There pil-low your
blue eyes close tight, Bright an-gels are near, So sleep with-out

head. If God will you shall wake, When the morn-ing's light
fear. They will guard you from harm, With the dream-land's sweet

breaks, If God will you shall wake, When the morn-ing's light breaks.
charm, They will guard you from harm, With the dream-land's sweet charm.

Evening Prayer

from *Hänsel und Gretel*

English text by
Hansel Powell

Engelbert Humperdinck
1854–1921

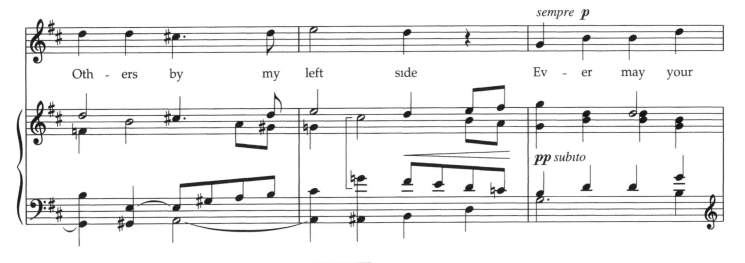

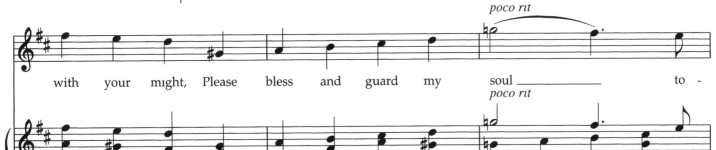

The False Prophet

Reginald V. Darow

John Prindle Scott
1877-1932

Allegro moderato

One June morn-ing through the mead-ow go-ing

Dor-is found a lit-tle dai-sy grow-ing, Bloom-ing there,

white and fair, nod-ding in the pleas-ant sum-mer air,

"Tell me, dai - sy, quick-ly, tru-ly tell, ___ if my dear one

loves _ me _ well. Will he be true till life is done?"

Then she plucked the pet - als, one by one. "He loves me! He

loves me not!" (a - las, to be de - sert - ed is love's sor - est smart!) He

The Lilac Tree

text by the composer

George H. Gartlin
1882-1963

girl drew back in great sur-prise, "You're a strang-er sir," said she, "And

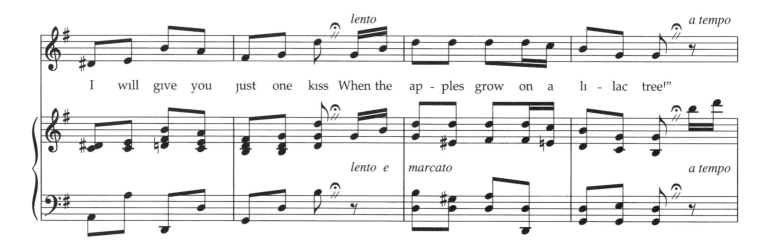

lento   *a tempo*

I will give you just one kiss When the ap-ples grow on a li-lac tree!"

lento e marcato   *a tempo*

The

boy felt ver-y sad at heart, She was the on-ly one, The

girl felt quite re - morse - ful At the ter - ri - ble wrong she had

done. So bright and ear - ly on the ver - y next morn, He was

quite sur - prised to see His lit - tle sweet - heart

stand - ing in the gar - den Ty - ing ap - ples on a li - lac tree.

Florian's Song
(Chanson de Florian)

J.P. Claris de Florian
English text by
Laura M. Underwood

Benjamin Godard
1849-1895

Allegretto

If there's a shep-herd in your par - ish,

A shep-herd charm-ing, good and kind, To whom at

once your heart's in - clined, Whom, long - er known, still more you cher - ish,

ff He is my love, Give him to me! *sostenuto* I have his

dim. heart; _____ my faith has he. *p*

p Are echo - ing woods his songs re - peat - ing,

Charmed by his voice, that sweet com - plains,

And do his pipe's mel - o - dious strains The hearts of maid - ens set a -

beat - ing, Then 'tis my love!

Give him to me! I have his heart, _____ my faith has

he

If, when there comes some need - y

Golden Slumbers

English folksong, 17th century
arranged by Charles Vincent

do — not cry, — And I will sing a lul - la -

by Lul - la - by, _____

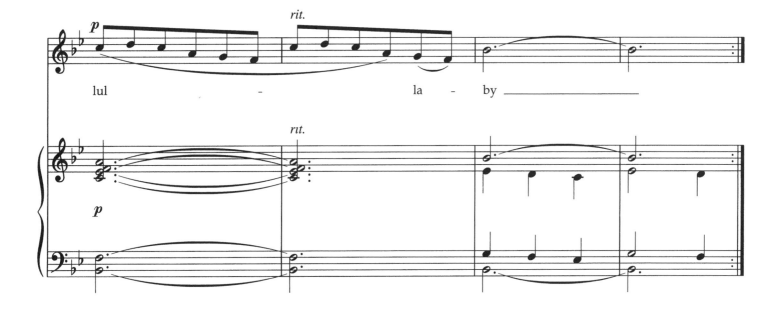

lul - la - by _____

It Was a Lover and His Lass

William Shakespeare

Frederic Austin
1872-1952

birds do sing, hey ding a ding, ding. Sweet lov-ers love the spring

This —

car - ol they be - gan that hour, With a hey and a ho, and a hey no - ni - no, _____

How that life was _ but a flower In the spring time, the on-ly pret-ty ring time, When

birds do sing, hey ding a ding, ding. Sweet lov - ers love the spring

And __ there - fore take the __

pre - sent time, With a hey, and a ho, and a hey no - ni - no, For

love is crown - ed __ with the prime In the spring time, the on - ly pret - ty

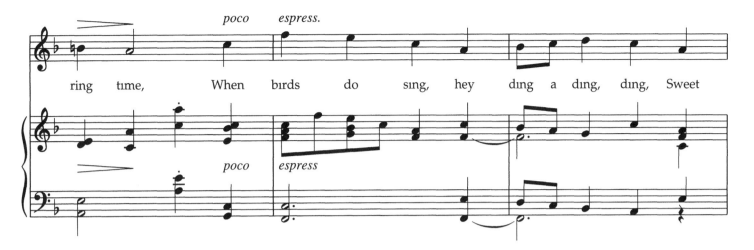

ring time, When birds do sing, hey ding a ding, ding, Sweet

lov - ers love the spring, sweet __ lov - ers, sweet __

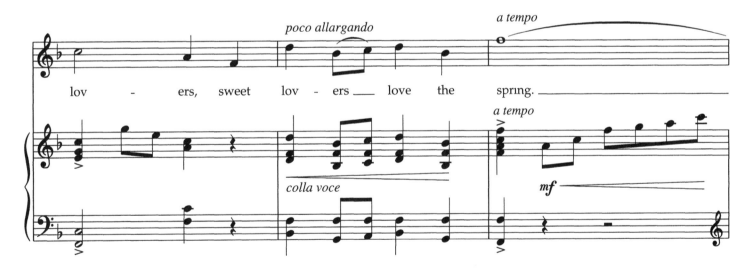

lov - ers, sweet lov - ers __ love the spring. __

Ladybird
(Marienwürmchen)

Anonymous
from *Des Knaben Wunderhorn*

Robert Schumann
1810-1856

1. Come, La - dy - bird, and __ seat your - self Up - on my hand, up - on my hand; Be sure I will not __ harm you, No, I'll not
2. Go, La - dy - bird, fly __ home, fly home, 'Tis all on fire, your chil - dren cry So sore - ly, oh, so __ sore - ly, Cry, cry so
3. Fly, La - dy - bird, now __ fly a - way A - cross the hedge, a - cross the hedge, The neigh - bors will not __ harm you, No, They'll not

The Little Sandman
(Sandmännchen)

from *Volks-Kinderlieder*
arranged by Johannes Brahms
1833-1897

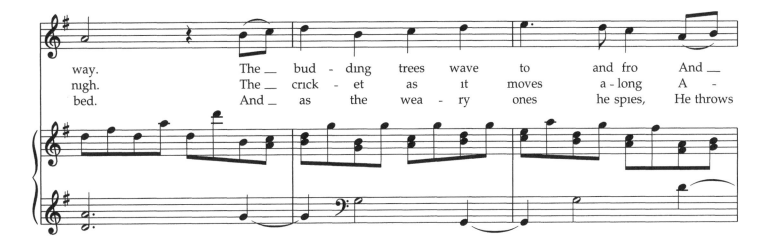

low ... Sleep _____ on! ... sleep _____ on, ___ sleep _
song. ... Sleep _____ on! ... sleep _____ on, ___ sleep _
eyes ... Sleep _____ on! ... sleep _____ on, ___ sleep _

on, ... my ___ lit - tle ... one!
on, ... my ___ lit - tle ... one!
on, ... my ___ lit - tle ... one!

2. The
3 Now

My Little Heart
(Non petit cœur soupire)

English text by
Joan Boytim

Jean-Baptiste Weckerlin
1821-1910

My   lit   -   tle
When   I   com   -

heart   is   sigh - ing   ev - 'ry   mo - ment,
plain   I   find   you   on - ly   smil - ing,

O moth - er, why am I so sad, __ oh __
Is there no dan - ger that you can __ fore -

cresc *decresc*

why? _____ My lit - tle heart is
tell? _____ When I com - plain I

sigh - ing ev - 'ry mo - ment, Tell _____ me, oh
find you on - ly smil - ing, Is _____ there no

cresc

decresc e poco rit

why _____ am I so sad, oh why?
dan - ger that you can fore - tell?

decresc e poco rit

Moth - er, you know, why are you not re -
Ad - vise me, then, the way to stop my

ply - ing? May - be you've sighed in your life just as
sigh - ing. Tell me I pray what charm can make me

I!
well? } My lit - tle heart is sigh - ing ev - 'ry mo - ment,

Tell me, dear moth - er, oh, why do I sigh?

The Nightingale

English text by
Charles Fonteyn Manney

Alexander Alabieff
1802-1852

Slowly and expressively

1 Night - in - gale, O night - in - gale,
2 When my lov - er went _____ from me,
3 Through the night for - lorn _____ I weep,

Song out - pour - ing _____ through _____ the vale.
"Take this ____ gold - en ____ ring," _____ said he
Wear - y ____ watch till ____ dawn _____ I keep

Ah, for - sake me ____ not, ____ stay ____ near, ____
"Think of ____ me, while ____ far ____ a - way, ____
And my ring! A - las, the ____ day! ____

You _____ my joy, my on - ly cheer!
Faith - ful I will ev - er stay "
From _____ my fin - ger slipped _____ a - way.

Night - in - gale, O night - in - gale,

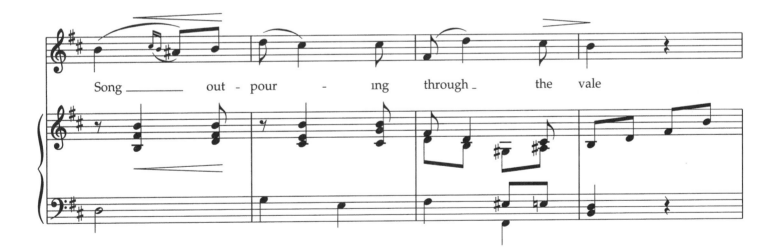

Song _____ out - pour - ing through _____ the vale

41

Oh! Dear, What Can the Matter Be?

English, 16th century

Moderately fast

Fine 3rd time

John - ny's so long at the fair. _____ 1. He
                                                 2 He

prom - ised he'd buy me a fair - ing should please me, And
prom - ised he'd bring me a bas - ket of po - sies, A

then for a kiss, oh! he vowed he would tease me, He
gar - land of lil - ies, a gar - land of ro - ses, A
prom - ised he'd bring me a
lit - tle straw hat, to set

bunch of blue rib - bons, To tie up my bon - ny brown hair. _____ And it's
off the blue rib - bons, That tie up my bon - ny brown hair. _____ And it's

Oh, Pretty Birds
(Petits Oiseaux)

Honoré de Balzac
English text by
George L. Osgood

Henri-Joseph Riegel
1741-1799
arranged by Jean-Baptiste Weckerlin
1821-1910

Sing to __ the Lord _____ Whose good - ness brought_you to the earth, Now

cresc. *p*

sing ye birds of __ the spring and __ of love _____

cresc.

Sing to _____ the Lord _____ Whose

p

good - ness brought __ you to the earth, Now

sing ye birds of __ the spring and __ of love, _____ Now

sing ye _____ birds _____ of __ the spring ___ and __ of love. _____

And

now from all _____ choose a dain - ty __ bird - ling,

And by __ your songs _____ at-tempt her heart _ to move, _____

To that _ sweet bird _____ re-peat it, nev-er end-ing, That

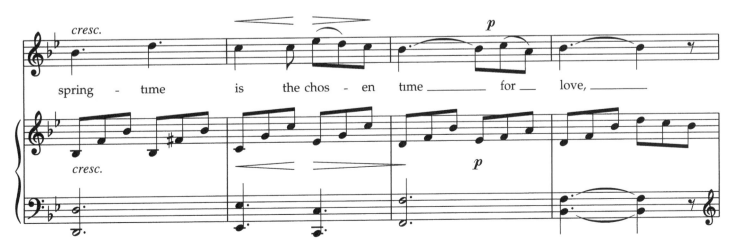

spring - time is the chos - en time _____ for _ love, _____

To that _____ sweet bird _____ re -

peat it nev - er end - ing That

spring - time is the chos - en time _____ for ___ love, _____ That

spring - time is the chos - en time _____ for ___ love.

The Winter It Is Past

vv. 1 & 2 Robert Burns
vv. 3 & 4 anonymous

melody from *Johnson's Museum*
arranged by Helen Hopekirk
1856-1945

Simply

1 The __
2. The __

win — ter it is past, and the sum — mer's come at last, And the
rose up — on the brier, by the wa — ter's run — ning clear, May have

small __ birds __ sing on ev — 'ry tree; _____ The __
charms __ for the lin — net or the bee; _____ Their __

hearts of these are glad, but ___ mine is ver - y sad, For my
lit - tle loves are blest, their ___ lit - tle hearts at rest, But my

true love is part - ed from me _____
true love is part - ed from me _____

3 My ___
4 All ___

love is like the sun that ___ in the sky doth run, For ___
you that are in love, and ___ can - not it re - move, I ___

ev - er as con - stant and true, But ___
pit - y the pains ___ you en - dure, For ex -

his is like the moon that ___ wan - ders up and down, And ___
per - ience makes me know your ___ hearts are full of woe, A ___

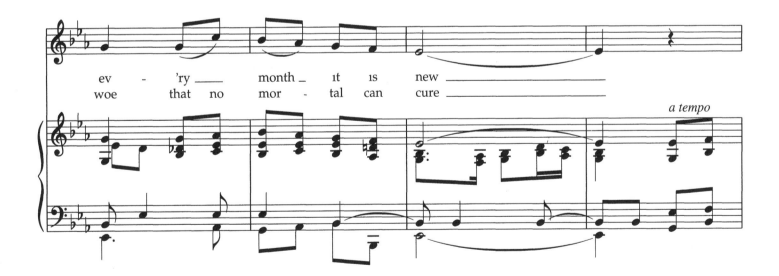

ev - 'ry ___ month it is new ___
woe that no mor - tal can cure ___

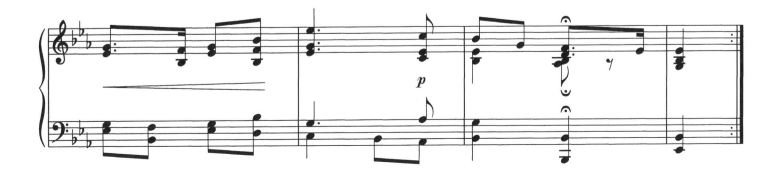

The Rosebush
(Der Rosenstock)

English text by
Paul England

Friedrich Heinrich Himmel
1765-1814

Sweetly and tenderly

1. I
2. And
3. "My

would that my love ___ were a rose - bush in bloom! I'd set him so
while in the dawn ___ and the dusk of the hours I che - rished its
daugh - ter what ails thee?" my ___ moth - er might say, "Thy cheeks are as

ten - der - ly here in my ___ room, Where through the wide case - ment the
blos - soms with fresh - e - ning ___ showers, A whis - per would rise, as I
red as the ris - ing of ___ day!" I'd an - swer, "Dear Moth - er, the

soft bree - zes play. I'd watch him and sing to him all the long ___
bent o'er my tree, "I love thee, my dar - ling, and all dost thou love ___
rose is to blame, He breathed on my cheeks and has left them a -

poco più mosso

day Where through the wide case - ment the soft bree - zes play, ____ I'd ___
me?" A whis - per would rise as I bent o'er my tree, ____ "I ___
flame." I'd an - swer, "Dear Moth - er, the rose is to blame, ____ He ___

colla parte

watch ___ him ___ and ___ sing ___ to ___ him ___ all ___ the ___ long ___
love ___ thee, ___ my ___ dar - ling ___ and ___ dost ___ thou ___ love ___
breathed ___ on ___ my ___ cheeks ___ and ___ has ___ left ___ them ___ a -

day.
me?"
flame."

The Sweetest Flower that Blows

Frederic Peterson

Charles B. Hawley
1858-1915

The sweet-est flow'r that blows I give you as we part, For

you it is a rose, _____ For me it is my heart, For

you it is a rose, For me it is my heart The fra-grance it ex -

55

hales, Ah! if you on-ly knew, Which but in dy-ing fails, It

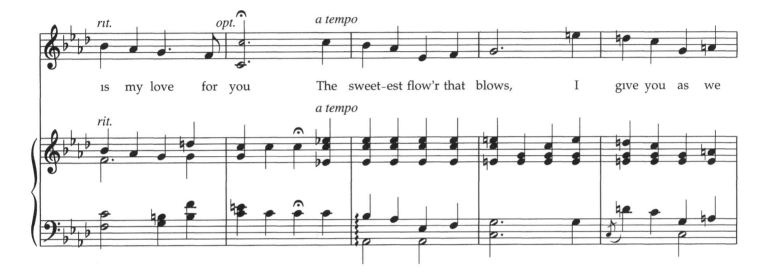

is my love for you The sweet-est flow'r that blows, I give you as we

part, For you it is a rose, ____ For me it is my heart, For

you it is a rose, For me it is my heart

Two Marionettes

Arthur Law

Edith Cooke

Two mar-io-nettes, the sto-ry goes, Once trav-elled from town to town,

She was a Prin-cess fine and fair, And he was on-ly a clown; But he

loved her true, As a clown will do, And ven-tured at length to

locks. "He I wed," said she, "must a no - ble ___ be, A

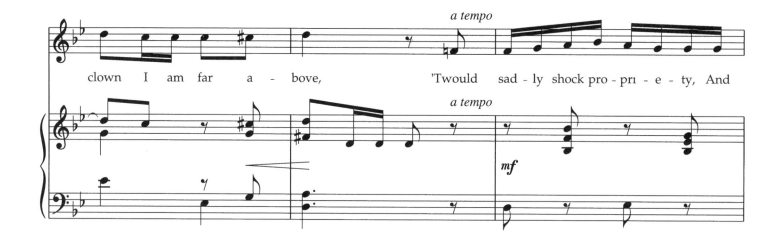

clown I am far a - bove, 'Twould sad - ly shock pro - pri - e - ty, And

deep - ly grieve so - ci - e - ty, And so I'm ver - y sor - ry, but I can't re - turn your love"

The show - man one day re -

dressed his troupe, And some-how it came to pass, the clown was ar-rayed as a no-ble Earl, And she as a serv-ing lass Then she looked a-skance with a ten-der _ glance, And said, "I am thine, sweet-heart!" He an-swer'd with ci-vil-i-ty, "I'm one of the no-bil-i-ty, And com-mon sense will tell you, that we'd bet-ter kiss and part!"

The Willow Song

Anonymous
adapted from Shakespeare

English, 16th century

Slowly and sadly

The poor soul sat sigh-ing by a syc-a-more tree, Sing all a green wil-low; Her hand on her bos-om, her head ____ on her knee, Sing

wil-low, wil-low, wil-low, wil - low! Sing wil-low, wil-low, wil-low, wil - low my

gar - land shall be, Sing all a green wil - low, wil - low, wil-low,

wil - low! Sing all a green _ wil - low my gar - land shall

be

The Willow Tree
(Die Linde im Thal)

English text by
Joan Boytim

melody from
Berg & Newber, *68 Lieder*, 1549
arranged by Heinrich Reimann
1850-1906

3. And as I woke from slum - ber, My

plea - sure all was gone Was no - thing there but

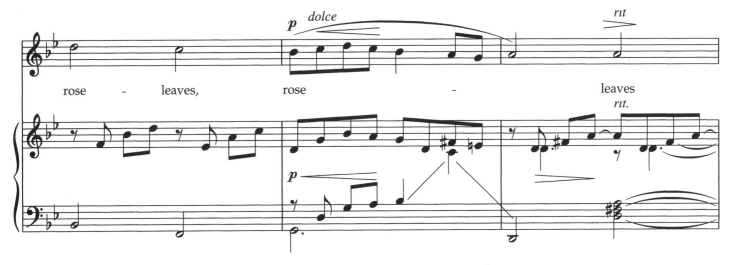

rose - leaves, rose - leaves

That light - ly on my face had blown